psalms

151-300

psalms
151-300

CHARLES H. HARPER

LUCAS
PARK
BOOKS

ST. LOUIS, MISSOURI

Printed in the United States of America.

In Memoriam

Patricia

1935 - 2017

and for
this great host of other companions
who have been my dialogue partners
in the joyful quest for human meaning

ACKNOWLEDGEMENTS

Some poems in this collection have been previously published in the following journals: *the Aurorean, The Lyric, Penwood Review, The Avocet*, and *Reflections*, a journal of Yale Divinity School. I thank the editors of these journals for their interest and encouragement over the six years of this book's progress from inception to the volume you now hold in your hands.

The cover art is from a lithograph by Roger Lersy that has been in my home for fifty years. Cover design is by Dawn MacKechnie of Powder Horn Press.

My daughter, Kristin, proofread these psalms. In addition to questioning some dubious spelling and punctuation, she also made several syntactical suggestions that improved the clarity and rhythm of individual poems.

Bob Rogers is a friend of over fifty years; also a witty theological interlocutor with whom I have spent many hours pondering life's mysteries while also enjoying a mutual passion for single malt Scotch. He has a deep knowledge of me and my poetry. His Preface provides the reader an insightful introduction to these new psalms.

During the several years of this book's creation, it has been my privilege to be a member of two writing groups: the Tidepool Poets in Plymouth, Massachusetts, and the Thursday Poetry Workshop in Las Cruces, New Mexico. The insight, support and critiques of these fellow poets have contributed, directly and indirectly, to whatever merit may be found in this poetry collection.

I have spent my entire life within the institutional church. During my mid-teen years I began to discern some disconnect between "orthodoxy" and my personal religious experience. In college I acquired crucial intellectual tools to help me think critically about all aspects of life, including religion. Those tools were honed during four years of seminary training, and the subsequent thirty-nine years of my pastoral ministry in Boston. As a result, my religious persuasions are always provisional and in flux. I am attuned to the Greek philosopher, Heraclitus (535-475 BCE), who believed "change" constitutes the essence of the Universe. We mortals are poignantly aware of our personal transience – conception, birth, life, death. History and Archeology provide a record of this same process for human institutions and cultures. On a far vaster scale, Cosmology tells the same story about stars and galaxies. All is flux. The poems in this book reflect my core celebrations, questions, agonies and persuasions NOW, as I commence my eighty-fourth year on planet Earth.

Sometime soon, perhaps tomorrow, one of my dialogue partners is sure to ask, "How have your mind and heart changed since you wrote these psalms?"

Charles H. Harper
August 26, 2018

PREFACE

From antiquity humankind has created psalms - paeans of praise - to reach out to the infinite, to that mysterious and ineffable Mystery that transcends our human reference. In the latest volume of Charles Harper's odyssey - his sixth published work - this contemporary seeker has chosen to use the traditional biblical genre as the vehicle for his ongoing reflections on life's meaning. While Harper imitates the sacred canon in creating an additional 150 canticles, he does not follow either the traditional format or specific themes of biblical psalmody. However many of the poems are cross-referenced with biblical passages as well as sacred writing from other religious or philosophical traditions.

Previous volumes of poetry by this gifted author were shaped by the craggy shores of New England. This volume reflects the southwestern vistas of Las Cruces, New Mexico where Harper now resides. The grandeur of the West enters into his imagery and consciousness. For example, the reader will find numerous references to the vastness of the sky for which the "Land of Enchantment" is well known. Psalm 214 concludes, *I gaze at the heavens/luminous/ablaze with stars/billions of miles away/their light touching me.*

Spiritually, Harper describes himself as "an agnostic Christian mystic," and believes his psalms "move in an ellipse around theist and humanist poles." He is a post-modern thinker who still values the rational scientific perspective of Modernism as well as the enchantment of the Pre-Modern era, although he necessarily eschews a religious dogmatism. *Thus we tell our stories, sing/our songs and lift our prayers/to an unknown god* (Ps. 230). Or in Psalm 162, *Let us praise artists,/scientists, prophets and seers/today, those whose names/we know and those we don't.* All human searching is valid source to *teach us/ humility in face of Mystery.*

"Mystery" and "Awe" are dominant motifs throughout. One is reminded of Rudolf Otto's category of the "Numinous" (*The Idea of the Holy*) when Harper invokes the unity found in "Inscrutable Mystery" (Ps. 181) or is muted in the presence of "Holiness" (Ps. 221).

These poems affirm an undergirding spiritual expression in all humanity: the idea that human yearning for meaning and purpose has no cultural or ethnic boundaries. Hence, while particularism of a specific religious or philosophical tradition is disavowed, a deep abiding universalism undergirds all. *Mystery/deep mystery/ far/ beyond where sacred texts can go* (Ps. 161) or *Great Mystery/we acknowledge the limits/of our metaphors/Yet in our many languages/we sing your many names* (Ps. 164).

How are these poems to be enjoyed? They can be accomplices to daily meditations or devotions; they are equally useful for the occasional savoring. There is no internal arrangement according to theme, though an index of recurring motifs is found at the back of the book. Each reader will develop a favorite way of accessing the riches offered by this southwestern poet. As an introduction to the immense span of Charles Harper's poetic grace and imagination, my own personal favorite is Psalm 177.

This is a worthy "Chapter Six" to Harper's prior collections. It represents the latest update to the poet's own journey – prophetic, poignantly personal, profound always. As such it is uniquely particular. Yet the one who is an active seeker will find a compelling companion walking apace alongside his or her own path of life. The thoughtful pilgrim will read and re-read, finding new meaning with each perusal, adding one's own distinctive "Amen" to the dialogic encounter. The final poem in this volume begins, *Ten thousand psalms chant/dance and sing within/I have spoken a few/and need not weary you with more/These songs are also in you.* But Harper need not be concerned that he may weary us by continuing beyond Psalm 300. Indeed, we will look forward to his future poetic offerings. His soul music draws us more deeply into our own.

Robert Rogers
April 27, 2018

Robert Rogers is Emeritus Professor of Religion, Hampden-Sydney College

Psalm 151

As far back as memory goes,
and farther, I've heard this music

It hummed in my mother's womb
and in her mother's . . .

It thunders in quadruple fortissimo
shaking me to the depth

It whispers in triple pianissimo
fading into silence

Its countless moods and variations
call up harmonies and dissonances

that confound my quest
for a unifying theme – except

It Is

A life-time ago the Muse said
find words for what you hear

Whether a trick on me
or blessing is hard to say

An impossible assignment,
a life's work

searching for language
to tell you what I hear

Former things have past.
New things I now declare.
Before they spring forth
I tell you of them.
Sing to the Lord a new song
Isaiah 42: 9-10

Psalm 152

High Mystery,
did you arrange the Universe thus
with all of its intricate workings?
Or did it arrange itself?
Is there a difference?
Is this all from you?
Or are you All?

Like a small child
my questions are endless –
but I do not expect an answer
nor do I want one

Were you to address me
in the language I know
you would be less than I imagine,
far less than I desire

Your silence
your darkness
your absence
hold me in their thrall

My thoughts are not your thoughts,
nor my ways your ways
Isaiah 55: 8

Psalm 153

Monumental moment!
Now, here, alive –
you, me, all of us
on this emerald planet
spinning around its small star,
one among a billion billion
flaming orbs – all of them
together mere flicker of candle
against the vast darkness,
the impenetrable mystery
toward whom we reach
and reach and reach
in art and song,
in poetry and longing,
in science and imagination,
in generosity and compassion

Impenetrable darkness
wooing us
here and there
now and then
with intuitive flashes
of light and beauty

Monumental moments!

Let all who take refuge in you rejoice,
let them ever sing for joy
Psalm 5: 11

Psalm 154

You seem
unapproachable light
impenetrable darkness
intriguing mystery
profound silence
palpable presence

I have only human language
to speak of you –
to speak of that which is beyond
mortal word and mind

Yet, I pray
with words –
sparingly
humbly
perhaps foolishly

Most often
silence seems best –
listening
the truest form of prayer

A time to keep silence, and a time to speak
Ecclesiastes 3: 7

Psalm 155

Life,
animate/inanimate,
subatomic/Himalayan,
whatever size or speed
or other than the above,
the whole shebang
enveloped in Mystery

Today
one micro moment
in the immense journey –
perhaps linear
to omega point
or circular
on eternal wheel

or crazy
boogie-woogie
catapulted from big bang
in the soul and shaking us
awake –
Psalmic metaphors sing
in a new key

You do not forsake those who seek you
Psalm 9:10

Psalm 156

a humble man
who has much
about which to be humble –
a wise man
who understands
his position
in the Universe

Then God answered Job out of the whirlwind,
Where were you when I laid the foundations of Earth?
Tell me if you have understanding
Job 38: 1&4

Psalm 157

Sing
children of Earth

Look upon Earth
sing of all you see

Sing your wonder, your joy,
your lament and horror

Look out upon the Universe
sing

Sing your awe, amazement,
terror, curiosity and gratitude

Look into yourself
sing

Sing the mystery and surprise
of your one, incomparable life

Sing the joy and sorrow,
shame and goodness of you

Look upon your neighbors
sing

Sing their friendship and generosity,
their fears and needs

Sing their diversity and gifts,
their one humanity with you

Sing children of Earth
sing

Make a joyful noise to the Lord,
all the earth.
Break forth into joyous song
and sing praises
Psalm 98: 4

7

Psalm 158

Mixed choirs of birds
fill pre-dawn skies with song

Again today, Earth's star persists in holding
our small planet in its life-giving orbit

Laboring hands of at least a hundred workers
have brought me this morning's coffee

Hubble's picture of an exploding supernova
ninety-three billion light years from Earth

quickens my heartbeat,
as did the panoply of stars in last night's sky

How long, I wonder, can greed and enmity persist
in a Universe that bends the human heart toward awe

Two gray squirrels chatter and chase
each other through branches of oak and pine

Finite microcosms of infinite atomic connections
spark the Universe this moment, every moment,

pulsing the whole shebang onward
to a far, far future – beyond imagination

Yet we will imagine, probe, experiment,
question, guess to our hearts' discontent

until lifted, at last, into song and prayer

>   Oh Beloved, you're so obvious
>   you're hidden from our sight.
>   Rumi

Psalm 159

Thou
You
That
It
Whatever
Wherever
Nothing
All

Beyond knowing,
exceeding imagination

That Which Is

You who care for my small self
amidst the immeasurable vastness
of our Universe – or that which is
indifferent to my fortunes,
unaware of human life
so recently risen from the seething
chaos of creation

Grand process driving to stunning goal?
Random process of mindless fate?
Who can say?

Yet presenting Yourself irrefutably
to all my senses ravaged
by unutterable joy and pain,
wonder and awe at each birthing,
greening, budding, running, falling,
dying mystery that daily shouts
to me, *Look, look, look,*
you are alive

> O Lord, open my lips
> and my mouth will show forth your praise
> Psalm 51: 15

Psalm 160

Enigma within mystery
within darkness

Not of our flesh or mind
or spirit – wholly Other

Yet of us, of our Universe
inexplicably

How do we address You
who is not a "you"?

How does our species, recently arrived
on Earth, presume your presence?

Bold leap of imagination
never before surmised

We cringe at anthropological
metaphors glibly used for You

Yet this language is what we have,
our limit and our glory

Are we fools to believe we can speak
of what we do not know,

to invent nouns to name the unseen,
to reference You with our frail pronouns?

Bear with us patiently, Great Mystery,
we are on a journey never before taken

> Why do you stand far off, O Lord?
> Psalm 10: 1

Psalm 161

Mystery
deep mystery
far beyond
where words can take us,

when we reach
toward you
we tremble with awe
at your otherness.

We stammer
human words,
the only language we have,
to express the inexpressible.

Humbly we confess
how often we misuse
our words for you,
forgetting they are metaphors,

arrogantly attributing literal
meaning to anthropomorphisms
for the Holy, making idols
of our sacred texts.

Mystery
deep mystery
far beyond
where sacred texts can go,

we praise you
for luminous moments
when, stripped of language,
we stand naked

in your presence
wordless with wonder.

That which is far off and deep,
very deep. Who can find it out?
Ecclesiastes 7: 24

Psalm 162

Let us praise
those whose names,
if they had names,
are long forgotten,

our primeval ancestors, men,
women, girls and boys who first
trembled with terror before
nature's thunderous violence,

those who first looked
at star-studded skies arching
over their small camps
and exclaimed wonder

long before there were words
for terror and wonder.
Let us praise generation
after generation of nameless

ancestors who lived in awe,
terror and wonder, implanting
in the human genome
reverence in face of Mystery

Let us praise artists,
scientists, prophets and seers
today, those whose names
we know and those we don't,

all who open our eyes,
minds and hearts, widen
our horizons, teach us
humility in face of Mystery

Fanfare for the Common Man
Aaron Copland

Psalm 163

God
this is an awful job
impossible

How to write lyrics
compose music
out of absolute silence

Listen, she said

Commune with your own hearts
on your beds, and be silent.
Psalms 4: 4

Psalm 164

You come to us,
as you have come
to our mothers and fathers
before us, in ways
too numerous to count,
too wondrous to comprehend,
too protean to name

Yet we persist in naming you –
Zeus, Jehovah, Indus, Great Spirit,
God, Athena, Allah, Krishna,
Lord, Way . . .

Generation after generation
we give you names,
only to watch them wither
and disappear,
lost in the splendor of Light
or vanished into the Darkness
that is You

Great Mystery,
we acknowledge the limits
of our metaphors.
Yet in our many languages
we sing your many names,
grateful for our lives
within your sacred presence

What's in a name? That which we call a rose
By any other word would smell as sweet
William Shakespeare

Psalm 165

Your absence
hovers like a deep darkness
over me,

void
emptiness
nothing.

No one to hear
my complaint,
my despair.

Who are you?
Where are you?
What is this Nothing

that comes and goes,
fills me with longing –
then leaves me bereft?

Come, friends, circle me,
embrace me with your arms,
your stories and songs.

Light a candle,
walk with me
through this night.

O my God, I cry by day,
but you do not answer;
and by night, but find no rest
Psalm 22: 2

Psalm 166

Fascinated
by Christianity's myriad forms
and styles – and how each one,
with its particular slant on faith,
draws devotees through its doors
into life enhancing community

Fascinated
by the myriad ways the life
of a First Century Jewish teacher
is remembered, honored –
even worshipped by some,
anathema to his own piety

Over a long life
I have walked through doors
of various religious traditions
where my soul was nurtured
for a time—then wasn't.
I walked out

Fascinated
by the story of Abraham,
an ancient myth to which I turn
from time to time. More than once
he forged his way ahead to deeper
faith by walking out

God said to Abram, "Go from your country
and your kindred and your father's house
to the land I will show you, and I will bless you"
Genesis 12: 1-2

Psalm 167

Billions
upon billions of galaxies,
our small Milky Way being one

Scattered islands of light
drifting away from each other
in a sea of darkness so deep
we cannot comprehend it,
so vast we cannot imagine
its edges, let alone see them

Galaxies floating in a Universe
ninety-five percent out of sight,
beyond our knowing,
yet within our wondering
and longing

Oh, Magnificent Mystery
of origins, life and endings,
how wonderful are your works,
and your ways beyond understanding

The heavens are telling the glory of God,
and the firmament proclaims his handiwork
Psalm 19: 1

Psalm 168

Unseen
unheard
unknown to the mind
yet a Presence

You are
my great interlocutor.
No moment of my life
is outside your questions,

your questions guiding me
into more abundant realization
of who I am in this world,
questions pushing me

deeper into my Center,
this Center that is You/me,
questions that do not let me rest
until I rest in You

Our hearts are restless
until they rest in you
Augustine

Psalm 169

We sing of Earth's bounty,
all things necessary for life
are her gifts to us

The magnitude of her overflowing
abundance calls forth our wonder,
our thanksgiving, dance and song

Yet, we hear the discordant
lament of the poor and hungry
crying from ravaged streets

of war, greed and neglect,
their tears asking, "Where
has our species gone wrong?"

Their weeping turns us
to them in compassion –
or away in despair

The needy shall not always be forgotten,
and the hope of the poor shall not perish forever
Psalm 9:18

Psalm 170

What is this longing?
Who is this
toward whom my soul leans?
Whence this voice
unheard by human ears,
yet reverberating
at the core of my being?

This sounding Silence
to whom I say, yes,
a thousand times yes –
and know I am Home!

There is a God-shaped void
in every human heart
Blaise Pascal

Psalm 171

Storm ravaged ocean
from which I keep respectful
reverent distance

Black hole
into which belief disappears
re-emerging as poetry

Candle's faint flicker,
trembling light in terrifying
darkness of wars and greed

Companions, arm in arm,
supporting us on our journey
through grief and despair

Music of laughter
in moments of joy, or humbling us
in our hubris

Palpable Presence
silent, unseen, nameless, intuited,
evading all metaphors

God beyond all our gods

We will not fear though the Earth should change,
though the mountains shake in the heart of the sea;
though its waters roar and foam,
though the mountains tremble with its tumult
Psalm 46: 2-3

Psalm 172

Blessed are You
who is
hidden in unapproachable light
veiled in impenetrable darkness
inaccessible to our minds
beyond language and image

yet a palpable longing
burning in our hearts

Blessed are You
source of this burning

The angel of the Lord appeared to Moses
in flames of fire out of the midst of a bush
Exodus 3: 2

Psalm 173

I walk through deep shadows,
path ahead obscure

Mile after mile
no familiar landmarks

My map shows well-worn trails
but not this narrow byway

Exiting the marked lane
seemed the right decision

But now I am, if not lost,
at least an uncertain wanderer

In darkness and silence, alone,
I listen. Night winds whisper

I whisper. Together our voices
blend into music for the unknown

Abraham set out, not knowing where he was going
Hebrews 11: 8

Psalm 174

This body-mind-soul universe,
billions upon billions of electrons
sparking in me, moment by moment

Mine for a season,
not mine alone,
for you, us, all

We flower on verdant Earth,
garden of enchantment,
then are swept up

into clouds of stardust,
light from which we come,
with which we shine

today and forever

Intimations of immortality
William Wordsworth

Psalm 175

Radiance
omnipresent radiance

Dawn
sunrise
Sun arcing all day
across our sky
sunset

Splendor of moon and stars
onyx gleam of night sky

Radiance

Earth's spring greening
summer blooming
harvest's yield
winter's white rest

Radiance
around us
over us
under us

In us

Embracing us always
even in our darkest hours

Radiance

> Your burning sun with golden beam,
> your silver moon with softer gleam
> sing your praises
>   Francis of Assisi

Psalm 1 76

We sing the beauty of Earth,
nothing comparable in the known Universe,

magnificent beyond telling,
yet groaning with war.

War upon war upon war
throughout human history

as we have evolved from small tribes
to villages, cities, nations and empires.

Homo Sapien Sapien, singer, healer, lover,
artist, builder, dreamer – killer.

Is the fault in our genes, our psyches,
egos, politics, institutions, ideas, ideologies?

Whence comes this envy, fear, greed
and foolishness that corrupts our goodness

into crusades against our own human kin?
Can we be saved from ourselves?

We celebrate that small band of martyrs
and prophets who have been exemplars

of non-violence in our tormented history.
We look deeply within ourselves

to discern how we may be instruments
of peace. We wonder what will happen

on Earth when a great culture comes
to its senses, lays down its weapons,

risks friendship with all Earth's people,
embraces a holy madness that says "No"

to the insanity of war.

> Why do the nations rage and the people plot
> in vain
>
> Psalm 2: 1

26

Psalm 1 77

Vast Mystery,
you who are far beyond
where our minds can take us

You evade our logic, science
and theology. Sacred stories
from the far distant past speak
of your presence, but fail
to persuade minds steeped
in modernity. You seem
an outworn myth from antiquity

Yet, the hopes of our ancestors
for a world at one with itself,
their longings for peace and justice,
their quest for meaning and community –
these also are our dreams

Whence come these dreams?
From transcendent purpose
embedded in our Universe?
From deep wellsprings within
each of us? From our species'
collective unconscious?
Who can say?

This we will say,
dare to affirm,
rejoice to sing –
with our mothers and fathers
before us, we also are seekers,
pilgrims on a journey, followers
of dreams, children of hope,
weavers of sacred tales

> O the depth of the riches and wisdom and
> knowledge of God! How unsearchable are
> his judgments and how inscrutable his ways
> Romans 11: 33

Psalm 178

Oh, my God,
with sorrow I turn
my back on your name,
this name our ancestors
coined for prayers addressed
to the profound Mystery
surrounding our lives

Your name
carelessly profaned
by our own loose speech

Your name
diminished by populizers
who preach a god
in our own image, a god far
too small for our great yearnings

Your name
abused by partisans to sanctify
self-serving schemes

Your name
debased by use of sacred images
and music to advertise products
that do not meet our deep needs

Your name
exploited by ideologues to justify
terrorism or protect privilege

My God, I turn away
from this name, but not
from your sacred presence,

you, who in your awesome
otherness, is beyond our naming,

you who endow us with freedom
to re-imagine the unimaginable,
to birth a new name,
to sing a new song

Bring many names,
    beautiful and good,
celebrate in parable
and story,
holiness in glory
                Brian Wren

Psalm 179

A holy stillness
surreptitiously
settles over me
from time to time,
not when I seek it,
but unexpected
surprise

Without warning I am
embraced by this quiet
presence, calming my
frenetic mind, pulling me
into my center

It does not take me
out of the World's
mix of ecstasy,
hum-drum and agony,
yet seems a blessing
brooding over all
the contingencies
of this mortal journey

As silently as it comes
it goes

Be still and know that I am God
Psalm 46: 10

Psalm 180

Great Mystery –
greatest of all mysteries, You
refuse my childish desire to see
you clearly, know you surely.
All my reaching for certitude
is in vain

Every fresh encounter
with a friend, a book, a song,
a bird winging through morning's
shimmering skies – life itself
unfolding with each uniquely
new day – all this changes
me and enlarges my picture
of You

In an expanding Universe
I am on a pilgrimage
moving out, out, out,
in, in, in
toward You

You formed my inward parts,
you knit me together in my mother's womb.
Wonderful are your works!
My frame was not hidden from you
when I was being made in secret,
intricately wrought in the depth of the earth
Psalm 139: 13-15

Psalm 181

Inscrutable Mystery –
how strange to sing
my love for this absence,
this silence, this palpable
void, this longing

You seem light and darkness,
many and One,
many in One,
a drawing together into All,
a quiet arrival Home

People of Athens, I see that you are very religious.
As I walked through your market place and observed
your objects of worship, I came upon an altar
with this inscription: "To an unknown god"
           Acts 17: 22-23

Psalm 182

Finally I reach this border
where books have taken me
as far as they are able,

horizon where definitions
falter, distinctions blur,
words fumble their meanings.

Blue skies lift my sight,
green Earth grounds my feet.
Silence sings her music

of the spheres whose harmonies
hold me – like a mother's tender
embrace calms her distraught child

Wisdom is a tree of life
to those who lay hold of her;
those who hold her fast
are called happy
Proverbs 3: 18

Psalm 183

We come with words and music,
our highest achievements

You respond with silence,
freeing our imaginations to soar

In our freedom we give you
countless names, plethora of sacred

texts and theologies. We build
architectural wonders and more

humble abodes, all for your glory.
Glory greater than any one tradition

can extol, glory far beyond that
which all of us together are able

to conjure. We probe immense
distances of stars and planets

We take microscopic peeks at inner
workings of atoms and cells

The macro and micro of verdant
Earth, our far flung Universe, our

wonder-filled selves – all proclaim
Mystery beyond our telling

We sing your matchless glory

> I will sing and make melody!
> Awake, my soul!
> Awake, O harp and lyre!
> Psalm 57: 7-8

Psalm 184

Impenetrable Darkness,
after my long resistance
I am persuaded to find
my peace in your vast
cloud of unknowing

Too long I have tended
the sputtering flame of certain
knowledge – time after time
banged my too-eager brain
into boulders of uncertainty

Vast Darkness, how surprised
I am by the comfort of your
embrace. My days and night
are full of playful light as I
surrender my need to know

what lies, forever, beyond
human knowledge

God moves in a mysterious way
great wonders to perform
William Cowper

Psalm 185

We sing the earthy
beauty of this garden
whose paths none now walk,

yet multitudes, with prayer
and song, look upon
through imagination's eyes

We sing deep waters of Justice
and Peace, two mighty rivers
flowing through this garden

whose banks are lined with trees,
branches bent low, heavy
with sweet fruits of human accord

We sing this earthy garden,
promised land within Moses' sight,
yet beyond his reach. We sing

ancient Eden lost, our own failed
utopias, dreamscapes, visions – all
songs of hope for this wondrous

arduous journey through verdant
landscapes and vast wastelands
toward what may yet be

> Behold, I create a new heaven
> and a new earth
> Isaiah 65: 17

Psalm 186

om mani padme hum
om mani padme hum
om mani padme hum

wisdom compassion love bliss
wisdom compassion love bliss
wisdom compassion love bliss

we walk with the wise among us
while we become wise

our wisdom grows into compassion
for this beautiful broken world

compassion draws us into loving
acts of kindness, justice and peace

here and there, now and then, blessed
by a sense of Sacred Presence – bliss

(based on a Tibetan mantra)

I ask no dream, no prophet ecstasies . . .
but take the dimness of my soul away
George Croly

Psalm 187

God
whom I know not
whom I love
whose absence seems a presence

Lifted up
or struck down
your absence is the presence
in whom I trust

In my living
in my dying
my peace is found
in none other than you

Faith is the assurance of things hoped for,
the conviction of things not seen
Hebrews 11: 1

Psalm 188

Sing of exalted Mystery,
you blue vaulted heavens

Extol deep darkness,
you fathomless seas

Marvel at the teeming varieties of life
swarming in your vast waters

Sing, rolling acres of cropland,
as you feed the world

Tremble, verdant Earth, as ravaging
storms rage across your lands and waters

Exclaim astonishment, arid expanses of desert,
home to countless living forms

Rejoice, majestic mountains
whose grandeur lifts us into awe

Wet-lands and swamps, celebrate underappreciated
wonders of the murky and obscure

Enchant us with your odysseys, rivers and streams,
flowing forever toward ocean immensities

Listen to the myriad sounds and songs of Earth,
humankind. Let us blend our voices with theirs

in a ringing anthem of interdependence
and thanksgiving

You will go out in joy and be led forth in peace,
the mountains and hills will break forth in singing,
all the trees of the field will clap their hands
Isaiah 55:12

Psalm 189

Tether me, Great Spirit,
to the beauty of finite limits

I know the ecstasy, fascination,
terror and awe of looking far
into star-spangled heavens, diving
fathoms into dark ocean valleys
and probing deep into the brain

Farther, deeper, higher
than any previous generation

Yet I am but a wee child
in a vast unknowing
wherein unfolds the telos
of my brief years

As for mortals, our days are like grass,
we flourish like a field of wild flowers,
then the wind blows across it
and it is gone
Psalm 103:15

Psalm 190

I sing of Life —
your life, mine and all
life in its billions upon
billions of forms teeming,
pulsing, swarming in Earth's
wondrous ecosystem

No other world like this emerald
planet in the visible Universe.
No creatures but us yet known
who, by chance or design,
are able to lift voices in hymns
of gratitude for our stunning home

Praise God with the lyre,
make melody with the harp,
sing a new song
Psalm 33: 2-3

Psalm 191

I met Jesus
a few days ago

Early morning,
seated in my favorite chair,
cup of coffee in hand
and a book –
the ritual with which I begin
most days

The book's topic is Jesus,
an overworked subject
that nevertheless interests me

While reading I become aware
of a presence in the room.
It is Jesus standing behind me,
at the right arm of my chair

I lay the book in my lap,
sit quietly and listen
to the silence of Jesus

He does not ask if I am
born again or believe in God.
He does not ask to which church
I belong or if I am a Christian.
He does not ask if I recite
the creeds or read the Bible

This morning he is a presence,
palpable and unforgettable,
who asks no questions
and offers no answers
before he exits my living room
as silently as he entered

Your word is a lamp to my feet
and a light to my path
Psalm 119: 105

Psalm 192

You have no name
except the many we give you.

God, YHWH, Allah, Brahma,
Elohim and ten thousand others.

Wakhan Thanjka, Wakhan Thanjka
chant the Lakota people

of the Great Northern Plains.
Great Mystery, Great Mystery

they chanted centuries before
my European ancestors first heard

them pray. Believer and unbeliever
in me reach across the divide, join

hands, in one voice chant
Wakhan Thanjka.

You dance inside my chest
where no one sees you
Rumi

Psalm 193

Great Spirit
waken me

Let me not walk blindly
through this day seeing nothing
of Earth's endless beauty

Let me not walk dumbly
through this day hearing nothing
of Earth's ravishing music

Let me not walk numbly
though this day feeling nothing
of Earth's terrifying agonies

Let me not walk ignorantly
through this day failing to be guided
by Earth's vast store of wisdom

Let me not walk forlornly
through this day forgetting
I have journey companions

Let me not walk listlessly
through this day ignoring kindness
or justice opportunities on my path

Let me not walk thanklessly
through this day neglecting gratitude
for Earth's cornucopia of blessings

Great Spirit
waken me to wonder, compassion,
praise and thanksgiving

> Awake, awake to love and work!
> The lark is in the sky
> Geoffrey A. Studdert-Kennedy

43

Psalm 194

Deep Mystery,
Sovereign Movement
birthing all
that was, is and will be,

we study your ways
in stars, planets, galaxies,
universes and Earth's
cornucopia of wonders

We explore the human body,
probe the brain, ponder
the psyche and marvel at the vast
complexities of being human

Here and there, now and then
we rejoice to discover how
small pieces of this intricate
puzzle fit together

Yet, what we don't understand is far
greater than what we do. We seem
the briefest of moments within
a splendor of eternal unfolding

Why not think of God
as the one who is coming . . .
the Future One, culminating fruit
of the tree whose leaves we are?
Rainer Maria Rilke

Psalm 195

I sing the dawning of this day,
    the promise that it holds.
I cannot know what it will bring.
    The story will unfold.

Whatever comes of good or ill
    is not mine to control.
I will embrace the light and dark
    alike to shape my soul.

This soul is mine alone to build
    from what life brings to me.
Yet, I need counsel of good friends
    for wisdom's clarity,

companions of the day and night
    to sing the journey's songs,
a fellowship of pilgrim souls
    to keep each other strong.

I sing the building of my soul
    in company with you.
True comrades on this pilgrimage,
    we'll see this journey through.

My soul, the home of centered rest,
    though harsh the winds that blow,
a quiet place of sacred peace
    amidst life's ebb and flow.

This psalm may be sung to the tune, St. Anne C.M.
by William Croft, 1678-1727. In many hymnals this
is the tune for "Our God, Our Help In Ages Past"

Psalm 196

We sing the longing of the soul,
the object of its love unknown,
yet felt within the human breast,
a sacred place we sense as home.

Unknown, yet given many names
in sacred texts both far and near.
But what we feel is well beyond
what words can say or minds make clear.

Great Mystery is the term we choose
to name the movement in our souls
when we scan the heavens above
or hymn our thanks for Earth below.

We hear a music deep within.
Its harmonies heal our discords.
It is a love song for us all,
a better way than guns and swords.

Great Mystery, you are hid from us.
Our best achievements are so small,
yet we aspire to point the way
toward a concord for us all.

This psalm may be sung to the tune of
"Old Hundredth L.M."
attributed to Louis Bourgeois, c1510-c1561.
In many Protestant hymnals this is the tune for
"Praise God From Whom All Blessings Flow"

Psalm 197

Jesus,
I have spent a long time
sorting out who you are –
for me

I have pondered many sermons,
(some of them my own)
read some books
talked with friends and mentors
listened to the questions of my mind
and the singing of my heart

Over the years
you have been different things
for me.
As I've changed so have you

Today you seem an avatar
at the very core of my being

With each beat of my heart
I hear your counsel – *Listen
to the silence, pay attention
to all that is going on
around you. Do this
and you will discern your path*

Walk this path with humility

I bless the Lord who gives me counsel,
in the night also my heart instructs me
Psalm 16: 7

Psalm 198

In the beginning
was the song

The song was
without words

The song is everywhere
and in everything

It thunders
in exploding stars

It sparks
in the atom's electron

It dances
in the jiggle of each cell

Winds rustle the song
through Earth's leaves and grasses

The song lifts all winged creatures
who give it countless variations

It runs with the gazelle
and the lion who hunts the gazelle

It rejoices in the peace maker
and weeps within the warrior

The song blesses all that is
It blesses poets

baffles them
eludes their finest words

Come before God's presence with singing
Psalm 100: 2

Psalm 199

Life –
mystery
stunning
unfathomable
challenging
humbling
brief

Prayer
my posture in face of Mystery

Poetry
my mode of prayer

Thousand foot carillon
radiant in the setting sun,
tolls its prayers
across the valley
to the next Himalayan range
rising to seventeen thousand feet

Tower
bells
prayers –
dwarfed
by these mountains

Mountains dwarfed
by sacred intuition

My heart is glad and my soul rejoices.
My body also dwells secure.
You show me the path of life
Psalm 16: 9,11

Psalm 200

Gratitude for Life
finding expression
in deeds –

acts
of nurture   amen
empathy   amen
consideration   amen
beauty   amen
truthfulness   amen
creativity   amen
recognition   amen
compassion   amen
thoughtfulness   amen
generosity   amen
kindness   amen
love   amen
justice   amen
reconciliation   amen
peace   amen

Each act reciprocated
by expressions of gratitude –

words
nods
smiles
bird song
leafing of flora
breath of wind
purr of fauna
spin of Earth
burn of stars –
symphony of the spheres
sounding from the mystic
evolving heart of the Universe

Amen

Singers and dancers alike say,
"All my springs are in you"
Psalm 87: 7

Psalm 201

Truth
for which my soul longs
is hidden in darkness

Darkness
is the teacher
who imparts wisdom

I commune with my heart in the night,
I meditate and search my spirit
Psalm 77: 6

Psalm 202

One –
How many ways to say this?
As many as there are
languages, living and dead,
on Earth

Learning to count, children
begin here. Learning to pray,
we end here long years later.
Beginning and end of wisdom –
One

This is the "hum" sounding
unfailingly in and around us.
Distracted, we sometimes fail
to hear it. But it does not fail.
It is the loom's whoosh

as our mortal years are woven
into the seamless fabric
of Eternity. It is the quiet
Center where discordant
jangles of human ego

resolve into a harmony beyond
naming. It is the deep well
within, from which we draw
living waters to sustain us
on our journey

Un, Uno, Eins, T'aari, One,
Hum, Home, Om

The Lord our God is one
Deuteronomy 6: 4

Psalm 203

Equanimity –
this is the home
where I will live today

Equanimity –
this is the face
I will show to the World

Come what will
of good or ill, I will draw
from deep cisterns of sacred waters

I will embody the Peace
I seek for Earth

You keep her in perfect peace
whose mind is stayed on you
Isaiah 26: 3

Psalm 204

There is no psalm I compose
no song sung
no shrine built
no good deed done
that your presence does not eclipse

For God alone my soul waits
in silence
Psalm 62: 1

Psalm 205

Our Minds strive
toward you.
Our sacred texts and teachers speak
of you

Our intuitions, deep
inner knowings of the heart,
whisper the Mystery
that is you

Touches of compassion,
acts of love
bring us into a Presence
beyond our naming –

Darkness
exceeding fathomless ocean valleys,
Light
exceeding high-noon sun,

who are we?
What is our place
within your magnificent grandeur?

Of old you laid the foundations of Earth,
the heavens are the work of your hands
Psalm 102: 25

Psalm 206

Vastness of my soul!

Familiar near horizons, then
the imagined unseen a bit beyond –
reaching toward far, far distances
intuited by prophets, mystics,
avatars and in sacred texts

Vastness of my soul!

I scan morning skies, horizon
to horizon, magnificent beyond
words, yet know this great dome
is a minute speck within endless
expanses of our Universe

Our forbearers tell us,
to save one soul
is to save a universe

Vastness of my soul!

You have made we mortals
a little less than God,
and crowned us with glory and honor
Psalm 8: 5

Psalm 207

It is good to give thanks
when your old god has died,

though your new god, if any,
is a vaporous hunch,

an insubstantial mist
without a name

haunting your heart and mind –
and may well be your old god

in a new guise for a new life
opening up in you.

Blessed be her namelessness!

Enter God's gates with thanksgiving,
and her courts with praise
Psalm 100: 4

Psalm 208

Vast and trackless desert
of greed and triviality.

No relief from rhetoric
of politicians, commercial

hawkers and entertainers
who would assuage our thirst

with gleaming chalices of sand.
Ancient riverbeds lie empty and dry.

Pristine cisterns are poisoned
by passionate ideologues.

Where in this anguished land
is there a green valley

where justice runs deep
like a mighty river

and peace pours down
like a cooling rain?

There are no longer any who are godly.
The faithful have vanished from among us.
All utter lies to their neighbors. With flattering
lips and double heart they speak
            Psalm 12: 1-2

Psalm 209

Where can I go
with this grief,
this loss,
this tear ripping
through my heart?

Companions, come,
be here with me. I know
this death is your loss also.
Together we will remember
and tell stories

We will weep and laugh.
We will hold each other
in our arms and hearts –
and in this embrace feel
the presence of our dear one

gone, yet near. Gone –
yet here in ways beyond
our understanding. Here
within the knowing of our hearts.
Together we will learn to love

in new ways. Learn to love
this absence which is
a presence, this one lost
to sight who still walk with us
in Light

My tears have been my food day and night
Psalm 42: 3

Psalm 210

In the beginning,
an unbelievable explosion

WOW echoes
through time and space,
expanding every nanosecond
with exponential speed

Great clouds of helium
roll and roar and roil
for a billion years,
then begin to give birth
to stars, planets and galaxies

Ten billion years after the beginning
one of these stars flings a fireball
into space, then holds it in its orbit.
Four billion more years pass
as this blazing orb cools, greens
and births life

One hundred thousand years ago
animate life on planet Earth
rises to its hind feet,
speaks its first word –
WOW!

Over ensuing millennia
this first word morphs into thousands
upon thousands of ways for humankind
to express wonder, awe, humility,
surprise, curiosity and gratitude
in face of unimaginable Mystery

wherein eternal creative process
gives birth to questioning, questing
creatures – who, with our telescopes
and algorithms, look to the heavens
and back to their origins where we hear,
unmistakably, the word that was
in the beginning –
WOW!

In the beginning was the Word
John 1: 1

Psalm 211

I have knelt at a thousand altars
erected to the Spirit of the Ages

My teachers are a thousand heroes
whose voices ring through the millennia

with myriad variations on one theme –
love kindness, do justice, walk humbly

with sacred Mystery embracing us all.
I am of this Spirit

I am also of the spirit of this current age –
young, experimental, discovering

itself, finding its way, at war with itself
and in conflict with the Spirit of the Ages

Yet, this adolescent is also imaginative, creative,
discontent, searching – and, in time,

will raise up its own heroes, its avatars
who, in a new dialect, with fresh

metaphors will add their wisdom
to the Spirit of the Ages

I wait, watch, synthesize, hope and pray

What does the Lord require of you
but to do justice, to love kindness
and to walk humbly with your God?
Micah 6: 8

Psalm 2 1 2

In the quiet of morning's
dawn I listen
to the thrum of my soul

It sings a language unknown
to me – yet, strangely,
seems a native tongue

It is a stir of silence
rising from deep reservoirs
of primeval song

It is music of stardust
becoming a one-celled amoeba
patiently evolving

into me – at this moment,
in this splendid morning,
trusting

whatever this day brings,
all is well

Whatever my lot, you have taught me to say,
"It is well, it is well with my soul."
Horatio G. Spafford

Psalm 213

We live in radiance,
we radiate radiance,
afterglow of the Big Bang,
our creation story

Where do we come from?
who are we?
Where are we going?

Our current creation story,
part science and part guess,
proffers answers to questions
one and three –
we are of the Universe's
ever constant Energy supply.
To this source we return
when our brief sojourn
on Earth is done

But who are we
now
during these fleeting mortal years
given to us?

Who are we
if not reflectors of Radiance
from whom we come,
in whom we live,
to whom we go?

God said, "Let there be light"
and there was light
Genesis 1: 3

Psalm 2 1 4

Late evening,
cloudless sky full of stars,
quiet moonlit landscape

Awe and amazement move
palpably through my body.
Gratitude finds its voice
in a soft hum rising
into nocturnal silence

I ponder words of Armand
Delsemme, physicist: "the Universe
arose out of the spontaneous rupture
of the pre-existing grand symmetry
of nothingness"

I recall the Bible's opening line:
"In the beginning God created
the heavens and the earth."
"Creatio ex nihilo", theologians
call it. Mystics of all stripes
name the Ultimate, "Nothing,"
no thing, that which is beyond
the human mind to conceive
or tongue to speak

Grand symmetry of nothingness,
a physicist's best hypothesis.
Creation out of nothing, theologians'
interpretation of ancient Hebrew text.
Nothing, mystics' best effort
to speak of the Ultimate Source

I gaze at the heavens,
luminous,
ablaze with stars
billions of miles away,
their light touching me

The heavens are telling
the glory of God.
There is no speech,
their voice is not heard.
Yet their words resound
around the world.
            Psalm 19: 1-4

Psalm 215

God –
with deep sorrow
I abandon your name

This name, one among countless
others employed to address Mystery
beyond comprehension, this name
by which my spirit has called
to the Great Spirit since childhood

With profound sadness I strike
from my vocabulary your name
debased, as it is, ten thousand times
per minute in this sad and reeling age

A name invoked to justify, nationalism,
terrorism, exploitation and political ideology

A name prattled by athletes who believe
God gives a damn who wins

A name used to bless ancient worldviews,
ignoring what science is teaching us

A name exploited by commerce
to sell a million inanities

God, while I walk away from your name,
perhaps you notice my use of other terms –
Great Spirit, Mystery, Presence.
I have numerous other metaphors
by which to sing my awe and wonder

Perhaps you notice, perhaps not.
Either way, I sing of transcendent
Mystery exceeding human imagination

Let the words of my mouth
and the meditations of my heart
be acceptable to you, O God
Psalm 19: 14

Psalm 216

The data is not all in.
I say this to my atheist friends
and believer friends alike

We are on an immense journey.
We are bit players
in a fantastical story –
unfolding

God or no God,
this Universe where we live
is of the stuff that blows my mind

Before our little ones have uttered
their first words, we should take them
outside on a clear night, spread a blanket
on the ground, lay them on their backs,
lay down beside them and whisper
to them of the billion stars and far
distant galaxies glittering above

Repeat from time to time

Before they can say "awe,"
they will have absorbed it

Train a child in the way
he should go, when he is old
he will not depart from it
Proverbs 22: 6

Psalm 217

Tiny pellet –
size of a ball bearing,
perhaps

Within it
undifferentiated Unity
unimaginably compressed,
everything that is to be

Internal pressure builds,
builds until whoosh –
miniscule pellet blows,
shatters

Original Unity
over billions of years
churns, expands, differentiates,
morphs into astounding multiplicity

Stars, planets, galaxies, black
holes, solar systems,
Earth
with its teeming flora and fauna
in mind-boggling variety
numerous beyond counting

In this multifarious garden
we thrill at our evolving story,
sing our awe, give thanks
for the throb of Original Unity
deep within the human soul

> Your stories are my delight,
> they are my counselors
> Psalm 119: 24

Psalm 218

In the beginning
One

From whatever
precedes the Big Bang
to this moment
One

As it was
in the beginning
is now
and forever shall be
One

I feel the throb of eternity
within – and am at peace

The grass withers, the flower fades:
but the word of our God stands forever
Isaiah 40: 8
First four lines of verse three are quoted
from the Gloria Patri

Psalm 219

Where do we come from,
how did all this get here?
Perennial questions of our species
from time immemorial

Priests, poets and story tellers
throughout all human history
have been spinning tales
of creation for us

Today we are mesmerized
by the Big Bang story
spun for us by scientists,
myth makers of our era

We marvel at pictures of stars
billions of years old, their images sent
by telescopes traveling through space

"Your god is too small,"
J.B. Phillips told us in 1953,
my freshman year in college

Since then, every time I see another
wonder photographed in outer space,
or my retina registers illumination
sent on its way two billion years ago
from a distant star, or I lift my eyes
heavenward into the astounding
light-show of a clear night –
then I know, no matter how much
my view of God has changed
and grown over all these years,
she is still too small

> Who is like you, O Lord, among the gods?
> Who is like you, majestic in holiness,
> terrible in glorious deeds, doing wonders?
> Exodus 15: 11

Psalm 220

Wings of morning carry this
resplendent ode to joy

Top-most branches of oak and willow
host a mixed chorus –

doves, starlings and sparrows,
at least twenty, their jubilant

cacophony of chirps, tweets and calls,
harmonic, perhaps, on the twelve tone scale

They sing a buoyant joy, also sounding in me,
a joy far more than changeful happiness

that comes and goes, depending on
whether it's a good day or not

No. This joy seems foundational,
like a jazz ensemble's rumbling bass

beat that holds together passing
riffs of gladness, pain, sorrow,

anomie, terror and hope idling
across the surface of my life

Deep
Abiding
Joy

Let the floods clap their hands,
let the hills sing for joy together
Psalm 98: 8

Psalm 221

Holy Holy Holy
Mystery within Mystery within Mystery
My imagination falters
My language fails
My heartbeat quickens
My mind surrenders
I rest
Holy Holy Holy

Holy, holy, holy is the Lord of hosts,
the whole earth is full of God's glory
Isaiah 6: 3

Psalm 222

I leave behind anthropomorphic
language for God, common
in popular piety

No more God the father
who loves, knows, cares –
is like us, but bigger and better

Paul wrote to his friends
in Corinth, When I grew up
I put away childish things

My prayers and hymns invoke
the Universe (and beyond?)
My brother's credo: There is more –

Hamlet to Horatio: There are more
things in heaven and earth than are
dreamed of in your philosophy

When I contemplate the majesty
of the Universe, its long,
long trajectory of creation

over billions of years, the dizzying
multiplicity of forms it births, minute
microbes to star-spangled galaxies –

then, mere moments ago, us,
each a little buzzing, blooming
universe in ourselves – Stunning!

Echoes of an ancient predecessor
psalmist: On this vast cosmic stage,
what is humankind

that we should have the good fortune
to be bit players, if only briefly,
in this grand unfolding drama?

> O Lord, our God, how majestic
> is your name in all the earth!
> Psalm 8:1

Psalm 223

I sing of the soul – your soul,
mine and all who, in an arid
age, dare sing of the unseen.
Soul – pulsing phantom within
the human breast, invisible

to our imaging technology, yet
evocative hypothesis, playful
conjecture that names tectonic
surges and quiet urges we sense
rumbling in our depths

Tell me your hopes and dreams.
Weep your pain, disappointments,
sadness. Howl your anger.
Sing of your intuitive leaps
over walls of accepted wisdom

Whence comes your compassion
for our World's suffering, your
courage to rail against injustice,
your resolve to stand against our
culture's illusions and isms?

Talk to me of happiness coursing
through your body when friendship
reaches deep, your favorite song plays,
you stretch out hands of kindness
to neighbor and stranger

Speak of these things – and I hear you
tell of your elusive soul, your center,
your essence – a soaring bell tower
of a thousand chimes caroling
the joys and laments that are you

To thee, O Lord, I lift up my soul
Psalm 25:1

Psalm 224

You
for whom I have no name,
whom my mind cannot comprehend,
toward whom my intuition reaches
but does not attain

You
who are inextricably woven
into the ceaseless births and deaths
of our Universe, in whom all human
achievement crumbles and is reborn

You
toward whom my heart leans,
whose essence is truth,
whose truth is beauty,
whose beauty is love

Such knowledge is too wonderful for me,
it is high, I cannot attain it
Psalm 139: 6

Psalm 225

I don't know
who you are,
what you are
or if you are

Yet there is that in me
which turns to you,
talks with you
and listens for you
in the silence that sings
my deepest longing

I seek you, my soul thirsts for you,
my flesh faints for you,
as in a dry and weary land
where no water is
   Psalm 63: 1

Psalm 226

Jesus, the Christ,
I did not choose you

You were a gift from family,
genetic and ecclesial,
going far back
on my ancestral line

For many years
I embraced you

Then came a time
to let go the "Christ"
part of you,
this mythology
accruing
century
after
century
layer
upon
layer
around the Jewish
healer teacher
who you were –

and still are
for me

Meeting Jesus again for the first time
Marcus Borg

Psalm 227

My religion, a roiling mix
of skeptic, mystic and agnostic

in which silence whispers,
"All is well. All will be well"

That we humans are here at all
fits my definition of "miracle"

That we war, abuse our planet,
connive against each other

rather than join hands for survival
and the common good is inexplicable

Yet we also compose music and poems,
create art, write stories, build cities

and civilizations, birth children, sing
our joy at the coming of each new dawn,

gaze in awe at night's glittering
sky – and cling to hope

Thus our minor earthly drama plays out
even as, each day, the Universe creates

new galaxies while also sucking burned
out stars, suns and planets into black

holes where they morph into new
forms of eternally constant Energy –

And here on Earth, where millions upon
millions of species have come and gone,

we homo sapiens now are blessed
with a brief role in this cosmic drama –

I hymn my gratitude
to whatever gods may be

I thank whatever gods may be
for my unconquerable soul
William Ernest Henley

Psalm 228

Where do we come from?

Perennial question.
All of us, from time to time,
wonder. Why?

It's the curious gene in us, the Higgs
boson particle, the itch, the irritant,
the intuitive hunch that lifts us up
into the sacred space of wondering

I ponder the question,
mulling over the plethora of creation
myths that come down to us
from ancient cultures. More recently
we've added Evolution to this collection
of stories

In the beginning a Big Bang

In place of God the Father,
creator of Heaven and Earth,
we now have the Mother
of all explosions!

Wonder and be astounded.
I am doing a work in your days
that you would not believe if told
Habakkuk 1: 5

Psalm 229

Life –
my life,
your life,
Life bouncing
all around us
in billions upon billions of forms,
a vast menagerie of wonder

Each here briefly

Even the towering Himalayas,
their spires piercing the clouds,
crumble and vanish

My little life, a faint glimmer
on the surface of impenetrable darkness,
an improbable blip in the seething
caldron of an evolving Universe,
an infinitesimal moment
in which to cry out
my terror and lament –

in which to hymn
my joy, my hope and thanksgiving

Catch it if you can. The present is an invisible electron;
its lightning path traced faintly on a blackened screen is
fleet, and fleeing, and gone
    Annie Dillard

Psalm 230

Dying,
dying all around us. More to come

I am trying to come to grips
with Earth's Anthropocene epoch
in which we now live, a new period
of our planet's history when human
activity is a major force upsetting
the stable climate conditions
of the prior 12,000 years

Radioactive particles and carbon
emissions blow into the atmosphere.
Overpopulation. Rising temperatures
and seas. Accelerated extinction
of plant and animal life. War

An impact on our emerald home
so profound humans may not survive

Darkness.
My moods swing wildly from fear
to anger to grief to resignation

Yet a hint of hope or faith,
or perspective – whatever
you choose to call it,
when you take the long view,
the very long view,
the fourteen billion year long view
of this evolving Universe

In the long run
perhaps it's all going somewhere,
and our species, recently arrived,
now plays a minor tragic role
in this spectacular drama

Thus, we tell our stories, sing
our songs and lift our prayers
to an unknown god

I found also an altar with this
inscription, "To an unknown god"
Acts 17:3

Psalm 231

I want my final word to be "Thank you"

An easy thing to say for one
whose life, though not without pain
and sorrow, nevertheless is blessed,

blessed with an inner joy
that elevates daily human pleasures
to higher plains of happiness,

a joy that comforts and sustains
during times of trial, loss,
doubt and discouragement,

a joy that lifts me from murky
quagmires of cynicism and despair
into which I often stumble –

As the words of this psalm arrange
themselves on the page, I look out
over vast Chihuahua Desert vistas

shimmering under endless blue
skies of an early October morning.
No wars are being waged here

Earth's abundance is shared,
though not distributed fairly. Poverty
pocks the land. Can this psalm speak

for folks less blessed with Earth's
goods than I? I don't know.
What I do know is this: the joy

celebrated in this psalm carries me
through good times and bad.
It wakes me in the morning, walks

me through the day, lulls me to sleep
in the evening. I want my final word
to be "Thank you"

In all circumstances give thanks
First Thessalonians 5: 18

Psalm 232

It took a while,
a long while, to decide
you are not,
at least not what I was taught

Still, you were not done with me
as you shaped yourself into a lonely
void within, an aching absence,
a sacred nothing, a darkness
blacker than a starless night

Though I abandoned you
I did not cease to pray.
The small flame of my candle
lifts its light and sweet aroma
into impenetrable Mystery

The fool says in his heart, "There is no God"
Psalm 14:1

Psalm 233

A terrible brightness
illumines the night sky

Syria is burning

Calculations and miscalculations
of nations, religions and ideologies
rain destruction beyond belief

In vain her people cry for relief

Only the dead find peace

Why do the nations conspire,
and the people plot in vain?
Psalm 2: 1

Psalm 234

One foot, then the other,
I sway from belief to unbelief,
seek synthesis somewhere between

My mind and spirit both thrive
in this middle ground,
their differences explored

by conversation, not debate.
Left brain/right brain,
intellect/intuition

Ancient homes of "either/or"
crumble.
Angels of "both/and" beckon

The golden mean
Aristotle

Psalm 235

God, if you are as unknown,
other and beyond belief as I dream
you are, perhaps you will not be
hurt or angry or take it personally
when I turn my back on you

Of course, what I am rejecting
is not you, but images from wild
intuitive leaps of my imagination
following ancient paths of mystics,
poets and sacred texts

Strangely, when I turn away from you
it is then I sense you near, and dearer than all
the broken images left behind. Today's newly
minted image must also shatter as I enter
more fully into your dark mystery

All the gods of the people are idols
Psalm 96: 5

Psalm 236

The millions of words I leave unsaid
add up to a pregnant pause,

a singular silence which, if I pay
attention, speaks to me wordlessly

in a language found in no dictionary
except that within the human heart –

Slowly I am learning to decipher
these sounds of silence,

humankind's original tongue.
Its vocabulary moves below the decibel

level of ears and beyond the brain's
reach. My heart hears and understands

It seems a simple melody within.
It slows my pulse and sings me home

For God alone my heart waits in silence
Psalm 62: 1

Psalm 237

Today
we believe
our Universe is expanding –
creating new galaxies,
recycling old ones in black holes
and pushing its borders far, far out
beyond sight of our powerful telescopes
or calculations of our best algorithms

So it is with my soul!
Amen

My soul is feasted as with rich food
Psalm 63: 5

Psalm 238

Great Mystery,
I move through life
blessed with an intuitive
sense that you are always
and everywhere present

This is a strange affirmation
coming from one who does not know
what you are or even if you are

Whatever you are or are not
is far beyond my comprehension

Yet, I will sing of your glory seen
in our expanding Universe, the slow,
tumultuous march of evolution
toward a future we cannot see,
Earth's spectacular beauty
and humankind's tenacious,
agonizing quest for fraternity

Hidden One, Alpha and Omega,
with humility and joy I hymn
my thanksgiving for this brief
moment in creation's vast journey

I am Alpha and Omega
Revelation 1:8

Psalm 239

I listen to the quiet
steady beat of my heart.
It is a drum-beat of Native
American wisdom calling me
to consider the impact of my acts
and words on the seventh generation

Seven generations –
175 years into the future

Interminable images on my 21st Century
screens assault me with news –
wars, contamination of land and oceans,
poisoned air and water, extinction of plants,
birds and animals

Short-sighted, self-interested calculations
and miscalculations of politics, commerce,
consumers and nations. It all adds up to death

I am of this. There is no innocence

The drum-beat seems a dirge, a requiem,
yet not without hope

A small voice, barley heard, chants
to the rhythm of my heart –

You and you and you – all of us,
if we can find it in ourselves to embrace
one another, then we will become the answer
to our prayers for Mother Earth

You shall love your neighbor as yourself
Matthew 19: 19

Psalm 240

I am not an either/or person
I was born into the clan of both/and

Both/and expanding outward from two,
reaching, in the long run, toward infinity

In the meantime incorporating many –
as many as my mind and heart, enlarging,

can take in. My knowing is broad, deep,
empathetic – and finite. Yet it is

of the Infinite. I am of stardust and whatever
lies behind the Big Bang that first scattered

this dust. Also, I am mortal – something like
Jesus, perhaps, whose deep intuitive sense

of himself sang, *God and human, mortal,*
immortal and reaching, reaching . . .

I am large...I contain multitudes
Walt Whitman

Psalm 241

Jesus is the answer
Perhaps
But what is the question

Deep calls to deep
at the thunder of your cataracts;
all your waves and your billows
have gone over me
            Psalm 42:7

Psalm 242

I sense a presence

a voice beyond ears
nevertheless calling

a scent not cataloged
yet a mist of perfume

a flavor missed by taste buds
but a sweet savor

a touch intangible
animating my body

an image eluding the eyes
though seen by imagination

a god unknown
except to sacred intuition

I am buoyed by deep waters
of unfathomable Mystery

A still, small voice
I Kings 19:12

Psalm 243

You ask
if I have been born again?
Absolutely. Many times
and more to come

You ask
if I believe in God?
It depends
on what you mean by "god"

You ask
if I am a Christian?
Yes, and also a Jew, Muslim
Hindu, Buddhist, Agnostic . . .

You ask
to which church I belong?
All of them
and none

You ask
if I pray?
Always, night and day.
My life is a prayer

Pray without ceasing
I Thessalonians 5: 17

Psalm 244

With telescopes and microscopes
I watch, with awe, Creation's dance,
at least its visible movements

With algorithms, research, imagination,
computer programs and guesses I hypothesize
invisible movements of the dance

Dark energy and dark matter –
ninety-five percent of our Universe
invisible to eye, telescope, microscope

Souls, gods, angels, energy, immortality –
unseen, beyond belief of my modern self.
Yet, during contemplative moments,

in face of Mystery, I find myself
suspending disbelief – singing
hymns of praise

Immortal, invisible, God only wise,
In light inaccessible hid from our eyes
Walter C. Smith, 1824-1908

Psalm 245

It could not be
a more devastating diagnosis –
except despair, hopelessness

At best
a few more months to live,
the doctor tells us

Odds are high death will arrive
far sooner
than ever imagined

Years before insurance
actuarial charts
predicted

I know
one does not get to choose
death's time

I ponder the finale of my life,
this brief exploration
on which I now embark

How to live
a full and fitting conclusion
all the way into the looming

sacred moment

Though I walk through the valley
of the shadow of death,
I fear no evil
Psalm 23: 4

Psalm 246

How can I not love you?
How can I not sing of you?
How can I not stand in awe
before the majesty
of these mountains
whose soaring spires lift my sight
upward into the brilliant blue
promise of this morning?

I shout yes, yes, yes
to this shimmering day
that neither hides nor reveals
the source of joy pulsing
through my body

I lift up my eyes to the hills.
From whence does my help come?
Psalm 121: 1

Psalm 247

My first word
this morning,
Thank you

though I am unsure
to whom or what
I speak

My second word,
I am listening

Again, unsure
of what or to whom
I listen

I address this Mystery
surrounding my day
by saying, "You"

My mother and father,
when praying,
used the elevated "Thou"

This sings,
but is anachronistic

My mind wanders
a linguistic wilderness
in quest of a better way
to invoke the Sacred

In an interim time
my heart hums,
Thank you
I am listening

Come my sons and daughters,
listen to me, I will teach you
Psalm 34: 11

Psalm 248

In dismay I survey the scorched
earth and desecrated sanctuaries
scattered across these wastelands –
the work of Your "true believers"

I cannot find words of sufficient
agony to say how sorry I am
that your name and credibility
are so grievously besmirched

If I, a finite mortal, feel this sorrow
so profoundly, I cannot begin to imagine
the infinite depth of grief into which your
great heart is plunged by this betrayal

I weep for You – for us

The envoys of peace weep bitterly
Isaiah 33: 7

Psalm 249

Sacred unbelief –
I sense a holiness in this unbelieving
place where I make my home today

This is a different address
than my former home with believers,
yet close, down the block a few doors

I've downsized, simplified, discarded
a lot of furniture, art, trivia and family
myth accumulated over generations,

all of it useful to earlier folks
on my family tree, but for me a clutter
needing constant dusting and explanation

Occasionally I miss the old house
and the comfort of familiar treasures.
But here in the home of unbelieving

I feel light as the breezes drifting through
its open windows and buoyed by the same
free Spirit, that in the old house, groped

its way gingerly through the accumulation
of beautiful antiques. A favorite painting
here in my new home is an ancient picture

of Jesus. It portrays the Jewish teacher
before the great theologian, Paul, and early
church fathers painted over the portrait

with their Christ

> There lives more faith in honest doubt,
> believe me, than in half the creeds
> Alfred Tennyson

Psalm 250

Immensity
sometimes felt within

It stirs
when I lift my sight
to towering mountain peaks
or gaze across far horizons
of ocean waves and desert dunes
or stroll among vast fields of stars
who fling their light billions of miles
to bless my night

It stirs
as I read ancient creation stories
alongside modern evolutionary theory,
or ponder the miracle of our brains,
each one a compact universe itself,
or engage a friend in conversation
that touches unseen human depth
where we most profoundly connect

Immensities
without
within
call to each other

My cup overflows
Psalm 23: 5

Psalm 251

This home of prayer
is where I find release
from my need for certainty

Here is the place
where my desire to know
what I believe vanishes

into mists of uncertainty
and peaceful acceptance
of what this day will bring

In this home of prayer
my longing for textbook
clarity gives way to trust

and listening

I will dwell in the house of the Lord forever
Psalm 23:6

Psalm 252

This morning, as is my daily custom,
I will spend time communing
with members of the international
society of the friends of truth

We connect with each other
in books, journals, letters, online,
and face-to-face conversations

We have no identifying garb
or symbols. We have no rules,
officers or dues. We understand
ourselves to be a threat
to ideologues and "true believers"
of all persuasions

Every day some members
of our society are killed
or otherwise silenced.
We continually update
our book of martyrs

Our unorganized movement
uses only lower case letters
in our society's name. We know
TRUTH, in some ultimate sense,
is beyond our reach. Yet we listen
to its silence – and sometimes glimpse
shadows of a mirage that hint of more

We are a people of John Keats'
"negative capability," able
to sustain uncertainty even as we,
with eager minds and open hearts,
attempt to live the truth – like
William Yeats who reminds us,
we can embody the truth,
we cannot know it

Oh send out your light and truth,
let them lead me
Psalm 43: 3

Psalm 253

I used to think the houses
of belief and unbelief
were two separate addresses.
You lived in one or the other,
could move between the two,
but not be in both simultaneously –

until one day, as in a dream,
I saw these two homes merge
into a single dwelling – my home.
In this house of unity, my prayers
are in a listening mode. I am taught
by the silence within me and beyond

Inner and outer,
one silence

That mind and soul, according well,
may make one music as before
Alfred Tennyson

Psalm 254

Where should I turn
if not to you
whose darkness is darker
than a starless night,
you who are hidden
from my mind, but sing
within the depth of my being,
convincing my heart
to turn away from despair
and put my trust in you

So much around me is amiss.
My world is not as I wish –
nor as you wish, at least
as your prophets have intuited
your desires and given voice to them

Yet, from your vast darkness
deeper than the sorrowful darkness
of my world, I hear singing –
        All is well
        All will be well

The deep one whose being I trust
Rainer Maria Rilke

Psalm 255

Oh, this shimmering morning –
its brilliant sun, its blue skies,
its bird songs, chirps and coos
blending into a hallelujah chorus,
its trees lifting their arms
heavenward, its cornucopia
of buds, blooms and blossoms
spilling forth into a thousand
colors, shades, and hues!

Oh, this emerald Earth,
our home,
no other like it found
in all the Universe –
yet!

Oh, the wonder
and the wondering!

I wonder as I wander out under the sky
John Jacob Niles

Psalm 256

Dear one,
you have slipped away
from our stunning blue planet
to make your home in another world –
realm of profound mystery,
void and silence, unknown yet imagined.
Far beyond mind's comprehension,
it baffles the furthest reach of poets' words

The candle I light for you
is dim reflection of the radiance
I have known in the sparkle of your eyes,
the lilt of your voice, your fierce and tender love
of all things mortal.
Yet the flame lifts my spirits –
and points my eyes heavenward

A new star is being birthed
in the skies tonight.
I give it your name

Lord, let me know my end,
and what is the measure of my days.
Let me know how fleeting my life is
Psalm 39: 4

Psalm 257

Your voice –
beyond hearing,
a sure beating of my heart,
a mist of breath
rising in winter air,
a silence calling

Whither shall I go from your Spirit?
Whither shall I flee from your presence?
Psalm 139: 7

Psalm 258

God,
I am placing my bet on you
though I don't know if you are
more, or totally other
than the beautiful construct
of my imagination

I know this bet
has no sure outcome,
even as life gives us
no guarantees

I believe
to bet on you
is to bet on myself –
to wager that my life
has purpose for good
in this hour,
and in a future
stretching beyond
my mortal years.
A future contained
in this moment –
this eternal NOW
pulsing in the heart
of my intuition

This NOW
whose silence whispers
Look, Listen, Love,
Be

> Happy are they who find wisdom and understanding.
> Their gain is better than silver and gold
> Proverbs 3: 13-14

Psalm 259

This morning's prayers
rise from a profound
discontent in the abyss
of my being

Our world is miserably
less than it should be.
The historical record says
it has always been so

Starving children, desperate
refugees. Self-interest trumps
common interest at home
and abroad. Terror, war . . .

Oh, unspeakable tragedy!
Is my abject discontent God's
discontent? Are my prayers
God praying? Are my prayers

and your prayers God breathing?
I don't know. I am in the depths
of Mystery – praying, longing
for what may come,

not knowing what that may be

Give heed to my cry,
for I am brought very low
Psalm 142: 6

Psalm 260

I look with wonder
upon this company
of fools

They dance in the rain
sing their blues
embrace the darkness

They smile through their tears
find oases in the desert
know no enemies

They forswear ideology
are at peace with uncertainty
celebrate their faith

Though few in number
they are found in every land
marching, singing, organizing,

challenging the powers that be –
Dreamers and happy warriors
they are a light to the nations

A light to the nations
to open the eyes of the blind
Isaiah 42:6-7

Psalm 261

To be rid of god,
this god who was a gift
from parents, church and Bible,

this god who is too small,
too domesticated, too much
created in our human image

To celebrate the freedom of sacred
Absence, to open myself to holy Void
and what may, or may not, flow into it

To struggle, and to settle
into the welcoming embrace of all
beyond my mind, my science, my imagination

To give thanks for the seen and unseen,
the known and unknown, the guesses, hunches,
hopes and questions that lure me deeper

I pray God to rid me of God
Meister Eckhart

Psalm 262

This singing I hear
seems a melody immemorial
stirring in the human soul

Or, perhaps far older than our young
species itself, a music winging
through the Universe on waves

catapulted from the Big Bang.
Or perhaps more ancient yet,
it may be the irrepressible

hallelujah that sparked
that unimaginable explosion
fourteen billion years ago

and still rings in all that is.
Perhaps, perhaps . . .
I do not know. I cannot explain

Yet I listen. I hear. I sing – though
my best hallelujah seems a dim echo
of this reverberating Amen within

A theology of perhaps
John D. Caputo

Psalm 263

Unless my eyes deceive
I see clearly
what is happening here

Mine is a familiar world,
today's routines repeating yesterday's,
network breaking news
merely new tweaks on old stories
of human progress and failure,
day after day mostly a mundane
tale of the ordinary – lifted
once-in-a-while by high drama
of love and death, win and defeat,
enchanting encounters with art,
nature, friends and strangers

Except for heart-wrenching headlines,
I am content with this daily routine –
interrupted occasionally by surprise

Yet, something seems missing. What
do my eyes and other four senses
fail to discern? What will give my
prosaic story a buzz, a fizz, a jolt?

I probe these questions deeply
with another question, perhaps a prayer:
what is going on *within* what is happening
before my very eyes?

How great are your works, O God!
Your thoughts are very deep
Psalm 95: 5

118

Psalm 264

I lift my voice, faltering
though it is, in a simple
melody of thanksgiving

My song, like a pebble, splashes
into the dark lake of silence
on which early morning floats

My music ripples outward
in a widening circle, perhaps
reaching other circles of praise

beyond my horizon. Many
voices rejoicing as the Sun
announces this new day

I will sing and make melody.
Awake, my soul.
Awake, O harp and lyre.
I will awake the dawn.
I will give thanks
Psalm 108: 1-3

Psalm 265

This pottery bowl
from the Earth
and potter's hands

These Wheat Chex
banana slices
and milk

This spoon lifting
their mingling flavors
to my lips

These taste buds
quivering
with delight

This body
taking in nourishment
and blessing

This breakfast nook
warmed by Sun
and gratitude

You have put more joy in my heart
than they have when their grain and wine abound
Psalm 4: 7

Psalm 266

I am pondering humankind,
how we have come so far
from the murky, microbial swamp
of our origins to where we are now –
a powerful species who, for better
or worse, is a major player
in Earth's evolution.

Oh, the wonder of our arts, science,
technology and gleaming cities!

Oh, the terror of modern weapons,
war, overpopulation, global warming,
consumerism and rape of Mother
Earth by unrelenting demands of Growth,
our prevailing economic ideology!

Oh, the wisdom of our philosophies,
spiritualities, knowledge, sages,
saints and exemplars!

Oh, the crushing sorrows of homelessness,
poverty, hunger, disease and starvation
on Earth whose vast abundance our species
has not yet agreed to share equitably!

How far we've come.
How far we fall short.

How vast our longing
for a world of justice,
generosity and peace!

Will we evolve
to this shimmering Omega
before we destroy Earth,
our only home?

> Imagine our power of love developing
> until it embraces all people –
> and all the Earth
> Teilhard de Chardin

Psalm 267

My prayers pull me
outward/inward
into possibility –
possibility of the coming God

The God who is not yet,
the God who is a call,
a beckoning toward what is
yet to be, a call that yearns
for my response – and yours

This not yet God,
when the time comes,
may elicit from us
a totally new vocabulary,
words for the sacred
beyond today's wildest
imaginings –

or perhaps not language,
but the breathless silence
of our wordless ancestors
as they hid their eyes
from the lightning
of holy Mystery

No one has heard by the ear
nor seen with the eye a God like you
who works for those who wait
Isaiah 64: 4

Psalm 268

Earth to earth,
we whisper over our dead,
dust to dust

Indeed, but it is stardust –
all of us, all of it.
Our mortal flesh from earth,
Earth itself formed from vast
stirrings, churnings and merging
of stellar stuff

This one whose death we grieve,
this garden where we commit
our dear one to the Earth,
our memories, tears, laughter
and hopes, all that we are
and will be –
stardust

Stardust
cycling and recycling
as far as we can see
into the star-spangled heavens,
into our grieving, resilient hearts

Behold, you have made my days a
few handbreadths, and my lifetime
is nothing in your sight
Psalm 39: 5

Psalm 269

I am thinking
the name of God
is a question, not an answer

This beautiful name
whose meaning evades our best
theologians and philosophers

This shimmering name
veiled in light
hidden in darkness

This evocative name
inspiring songsters, poets, artists,
cosmologists and other seekers

This name that relentlessly
interrogates our lives,
inviting us to move higher

This name we invoke
for comfort and courage
in our darkest hours

This name, that with a thousand other
names for the sacred, is indelibly
inscribed on the human heart

This name, that when we dwell
thereon, takes us to heights
and depths of our imagination

This name
that is a question,
an invitation, a call

Blessed be the name

The meditations of my heart
shall be understanding.
I will incline my ear to a proverb;
I will resolve my riddle
to the music of the lyre
Psalm 49: 3-4

Psalm 270

Ah, Life
Life with an upper case "L"

Your life, my life, our lives
all in lower case

Our little lives
within the Great Life

Our small candles, each
flaring briefly, then gone

Thus, in the same breath
we sing, life/death – one

The candle glows more brightly
in our eyes, its incense rises

more sweetly to our nostrils
because we know this beauty

is but for a moment. Ah, life/death
within the churn and burn of Life

Teach us to number our days
that we may get a heart of wisdom
Psalm 90: 12

Psalm 271

Calm in the midst of strife

Maintain perspective

Politics placed at proper level in hierarchy of values

Fierce engagement for short-run goals

Long-view moderates reaction to current wins and losses

Critical distance from all viewpoints, including my own

Disdain for demagoguery, lies and half-truths

Suspicious of all political rhetoric from my camp and yours

Contrasting life experiences shape our different political persuasions

Longing for constructive conversation instead of ideological debate

Alert for light shining through cracks of crumbling ideologies

Compassionate heart that feels the hurt, anger and fear of my opponent

Open mind trying to understand the truth as my opponent sees it

Listening for common chords sounding within our life together

Praying

The beginning of wisdom is this:
get wisdom,
and whatever you get, get insight.
Prize her highly and she will exalt you
Proverbs 4: 7-8

Psalm 272

Not rich
not poor –
enough

A few possessions
gathered over a lifetime
sufficient for comfort

Yet a treasure house of wealth –
wonder, awe, love and gratitude
adding up to ecstasy

A quiet ecstasy –
the silence
of God

The path of the righteous is like the light of dawn,
which shines brighter and brighter until full day
Proverbs 4: 18

Psalm 273

This ringing, singing, leaping early
spring morning

Tree branches, not yet leafed,
host a choir of song sparrows

A pair of cottontails chase each other
across brown expanses turning green

Forsythia's golden exuberance
proclaims the turning season

Goldfinches do acrobatic swoops
and swerves through sun-sparkled air

I, a creature among these creatures,
live and dance and sing

Praise God, sun and moon,
praise him all you shining stars,
praise him you highest heavens
Psalm 148: 3-4

Psalm 274

Ah, you chanters of psalms
old and new, you who sing
of things seen and unseen –

with our beautiful minds and amazing
technologies we probe the heights
and depth of our Universe. We peer
deeply into the human body and psyche.
Our telescopes and microscopes reveal
the intricate symmetry, complexity
and seeming chaos that swirls
around us and in us

We write our poems, sing our songs,
chant our mantras and dance our
celebration of this seen, tangible,
incredible Life

Yet, as we gaze outward to furthest
horizons or inward to fathomless
depths, we bump into Mystery

From whence does this all come?
Where is it going? Who are we who ask?
Our questions bedevil and intrigue.
Our curiosity knocks on doors
of the unseen, pushes against permeable
boundaries of the seen

We listen to the rhythmic beating
of the heart as it embraces questions
of the mind and gently leads us
into ever-enlarging Life

> Those who are wise may increase learning.
> Those of understanding may acquire skills
> to understand a proverb and a figure,
> the words of the wise and their riddles
> Proverbs 1: 5-6

130

Psalm 275

I listen to the wind
this morning

It rustles leaves
outside my window,
moves clouds
across the sky,
carries song
from bird to bird
and speaks to me
in ways no human
language can
in this hour of loss
and sorrow

It speaks an ancient tongue
far older than human words

It whispers,
Be still.
Listen.
Listen for solace
in your breathing.
Your breath is of me
and I am in your breath

The wind blows where it will, and you hear the sound of it,
but you do not know whence it comes or whither it goes
John 3:8

Psalm 276

Over the years many friends
have been my hiking companions,
but none so frequent or for so long
as Jesus

Some days he and I walk long distances
in silence, each immersed deeply within
himself, or quietly enjoy the variety
of cacti and other flora of this high desert
land where I live

Other times we have a destination –
an in-town park, a nearby mountain
where we have a favorite trail, a friend's
home, the local synagogue where we can
always count on a scintillating conversation
with the rabbi. Occasionally we find
ourselves marching in a protest rally

Sometimes we simply wander aimlessly
and enjoy each other's company

We have become close friends. Indeed,
we have discovered in each other a soul
brother. We see the world in similar,
but not identical ways. Though his
attunement to Life, in its myriad flarings,
is far more keen than mine

I have noticed some of his friends
call him "Christ." I never do

During a recent trek on a desert trail
I asked him about the "Christ" name.
He responded, "Forget it"

> He comes to us as one unknown, without a name,
> as of old, by the lakeside, he came to those who
> knew him not. He speaks to us the same word,
> "Follow me . . ."
>> Albert Schweitzer

Psalm 277

I struggle
to be in this moment.

My monkey mind leaps
from branch to branch,

restless, chattering its pleasure
and dread of the day ahead.

Eyes closed, a calm slowly settles
into the darkness behind my eye-lids.

Now – in this onyx chamber
a candle is lit, another and another

until in the flicker and shadow
of their flames, my eyes adjusting

to the dimness, I find myself
in a vast congregation. One close by,

recently departed this life, directs
her gaze and smile at me.

I know these people – friends,
colleagues, authors, teachers,

musicians, generations of family,
saints and rogues, living and dead.

All part of me, and I of them.
Oh, the vastness of connection!

Now – candles burn low, sputter,
go out. My eyes open to daylight

and shadow bathed in radiance.

Surrounded by so great a cloud of witnesses
Hebrews 12:1

Psalm 278

God,
I am singing the blues
among a people
who take your name in vain

I am lamenting the "God-damns,"
"Jesus Christ" and "holy shits"
that I hear constantly and sometimes,
to my great shame, slip into myself

But the darkest, anguished
rumbles of my blues are reserved
for the self-righteous pious
for whom you are a friend, a lover

of their kind, their nation,
and protector of their sacrosanct
ways. They have not listened
to your prophets. They know nothing

of your Otherness. They have forsaken
old psalms of majesty, awe and justice.
They lift eyes and hands to vaulted
heavens while singing silly ditties

of self-congratulatory human
projections – all in the name of God.
I hear death bells tolling. I do not despair.
I hold onto hope. I sing the blues

> You shall not take the name of the Lord
> your God in vain
> Exodus 20: 7

Psalm 279

Morning –
another day
to live within
prayer
gratitude
hope

This is the day that the Lord has made,
let us rejoice and be glad in it
Psalm 118: 24

Psalm 280

"God is the oldest work of art. He is very poorly preserved, and many parts of him are later additions. But that is the way things get built: by our being able to talk about Him, by our having seen everything else." (*Early Journals*, R. M. Rilke)

God is my art teacher.
Earth is her classroom.
She moves among her students
viewing our work. She comments,
makes suggestions, encourages

God is _ _ _

You may fill in the blanks –
or not. Your decision
will affect everything

As you move further along
you may want to erase, modify
or add to the images you've created

Possibilities seem endless.
There is no requirement
that you paint within the lines

There are more ways to you
than sands on the sea shores,
than stars in the heavens,
ways that lead to the Way
after S. Kierkegaard

Psalm 281

A sad and desolate place,
this treacherous wasteland
of Late Capitalism –
and crumbling faith traditions
born again as cheerleaders
for ideologies of grievance
and greed

Scant concern for truth
or the common good
is found in this age of Me and Mine –
except, perhaps in quarter-truths
of advertisers' slick pages
attempting to manipulate our desires,
or occasionally between the lines
of politicians' demagogic hyperbole

Is there no place to hide
from this desolation
except in shabby shacks
of denial – It can't really be
this bad, can it?

Hope is hard
despair easy
cynicism cheap

Yet – Yes,
a thousand times, Yes.
Ten thousand candles flare
in our night. By their light
we find companions
with whom to sing, to pray,
to party and to plot

You are the light of the world
Matthew 5:14

Psalm 282

I don't know about you and your hymnal,
but I have a love/hate relationship with mine

I love the melodies and harmonies,
not all, about ninety percent

It's the lyrics that drive me nuts,
not all, perhaps forty percent

On Sunday mornings, during the organ prelude
(dependably wonderful because it is pure tone

with no words) I scan the order of worship.
What hymns will we sing today

My spirit sinks or soars, depending
on what I see. Sometime the same hymn

can both lift and dash my mood,
its music shimmering with pure light

while a verse or two screech
from one or another of the Church's

dark ages. When we come to these
jarring lines I sing louder,

trying to drown bad theology with crashing
waves of my bass at full volume

Occasionally I wonder what others near me
think of this antic, or if they even notice

Often, as I move through rounds of an ordinary
day, I find myself humming a familiar hymn

No words. Humming

> Let all who take refuge in you rejoice,
> let them ever sing for joy
> Psalm 4:11

138

Psalm 283

I believe
there is nothing in our world
more quiet
than this butterfly's shadow,
charcoal gray,
floating
across my flagstone patio

except
the vast silence of God

given voice
perhaps
in my stumbling prayers

What no eye has seen, nor ear heard,
nor the human heart conceived
I Corinthians 2:9

Psalm 284

Pondering
what is deepest and best
in ourselves

An antidote to the grief,
despair and cynicism
I feel roiling my gut

as daily headlines batter
my psyche with impossibly
horrible stories

How can humans be
so venal, greedy and violent?
Why do we do this to ourselves?

This is not you, not me,
but it is of the human race –
our sisters and brothers

to whom, with tears and hope
(never-dying hope), I cry, *Stop.*
Look deeply within yourselves

Search me, O God, and know my heart.
Try me and know my thoughts.
See if there be any wicked way in me,
and lead me in the way everlasting
Psalm 139: 23-24

Psalm 285

Here and there, now and then
I hear snatches of our new story –
a story responding to an old question,
Who are we?

Our new narrative arises from the fear
and alarm we feel during this period
of Earth's sixth major extinction –
death of 20,000 species annually,
warming climate, rising seas,
vanishing polar ice, intensifying storms.
Much of this due to our species, all eight
billion of us, and growing, as we overwhelm
Mother Earth with our neglect, needs, greed,
exploitation and political failure

The emerging tale builds on old stories
of community – family, tribe, town, race,
religion, nation, – but takes these many
small circles and brings them, whole,
with their diverse gifts, into one expansive
circle of dance wonder and beauty

It is a drama in which each of us,
in our unique manner, takes on the role
of caretaker and lover of Earth.
This one Earth with all of her astounding
expressions of Life – in leaf and light,
air and flight, rock and flesh.
Now our nightmare of extinction fades
to a dream of fresh flourishing

Is this who we are
becoming?

Is this a post-apocalyptic vision?

> How good and pleasant it is
> when sisters and brothers dwell in unity!
> Here the lord has commanded blessing,
> life for evermore
> Psalm 133: 1 & 3

Psalm 286

Not what we do,
but how we do it –
how we live
from within our sacred center
whatever life brings

I am thinking about the young monk,
Brother Lawrence, who entered the monastery
expecting to spend his life in prayer, worship,
study and meditation –
but was assigned by his abbot
to do menial kitchen chores

One day, his hands immersed in dishwater,
an epiphany flamed – his humble task
was sacred work sustaining the life
of his community. In the kitchen
he was practicing the presence of God

At the moment, I am repenting the finger
I gave the driver who just cut me off.
My anger flared. I failed to honor the sacred
presence, the soul, within that driver,
within me – that elusive holy spirit
essential for a community to flourish

I don't know if practice ever makes perfect
I know I need more practice

Blessed are those who delight in the law of the Lord,
and meditate on it day and night. They are like trees
planted by streams of water that bring forth good fruit
                Psalm 1: 1-3

Psalm 287

When I die,
whether soon or late,
young or old,
I want to die in love

In the meantime
I want to live in love
with all that is vital,
mortal and transient –
and because it is dying,
I press it close to my breast

I want to die in the arms
of that Great Mystery
of which Emily Dickinson
spoke: *that love is all there is*
is all we know of love

I want to die in love
with the house fly,
the most distant star
and all between,

in love with my intimate
companion – and, as Jesus
counseled, my fiercest foe

I'm not there yet.
How long does this take?

Perhaps it will be said,
he died falling in love

Faith, hope and love, these three,
but the greatest of these is love
I Corinthians 13: 13

Psalm 288

Who would we be
without belief
in the impossible
improbable
unlikely
maybe?

Who would we be
without our hopes
for peace
justice
fairness
in a beloved community?

Who would we be
without dreams
of healing
for our broken world?

How will we get there?
This seems too large a question –
overwhelming
inviting despair.

How will we live this day?
A better question –
inviting us
each
personally
to take one more step
toward the unlikely.

Tell me, what is it you plan to do
with your one wild and precious life
Mary Oliver

Psalm 289

Who are you
to whom I pray?

you are All
you are One

you are the magnetism pulling
together all the puzzle pieces

you are the question who is
an affirmation – and visa-versa

you are the grief in our mortal journey
and the ecstasy of our loftiest hymns

you are this in whom we live and die
the One who lives and dies with us

you are that toward which we reach
and you are the reaching

you are on the way
you are here

you are
you

perhaps

The real work of religion
is permanent astonishment
Rumi

Psalm 290

God,
this name for you
is irrevocably chiseled
into my vocabulary,
my mind and heart

along with other words
we mortals employ to point
to the elusive Mystery
pulsing silently
in our souls

terms like Jehovah, Allah, Elohim,
Krishna, Spirit, Baha, Om –
and ten thousand others
by which we invoke the unnamable
river rolling forever into eternal seas

Yet, "God" is the name
my mother whispered, again
and again, in my infant ears.
So hushed and reverent,
so tender and yearning,
her prayers came to feel
like your arms holding me

God is love
I John 4:8

Psalm 291

Music deep within
bubbles up,
a spring of pristine waters,
quiet

When I tune my ears
to the murmur of these waters
rising,
music washes across my soul

Songs, learned and improvised,
find my tongue.
Joy – irrespective of facts.
Soul music

Rejoice always
I Thessalonians 5:16

Psalm 292

I am pondering all that is
lost to my memory

Surrounded in this room by books,
some read recently, others years ago

Many cloth-bound volumes wear jackets,
a menagerie of color and design,

bold relief against beige walls.
Books dominate the room's décor

Between their covers countless words,
facts, insights, guesses and intuitions

My eyes have seen it all, my brain
received it – but remembers little

Oh, I can quote snatches from Homer,
Aquinas, Pascal, Dickinson, Freud . . .

But what has become of that vast river
of data rolling past my eyes,

through my brain – then seemingly lost?
Or, perhaps sucked into a black hole

where it churns, tumbles, mixes, burns.
Then spews forth in a new synthesis,

an original story – mine

> Happy is the one who finds wisdom.
> She is a tree of life
> to those who lay hold of her
> Proverbs 3: 13,18

Psalm 293

You ask about God?

Let me tell you of joy
singing deep within me
as we walk together
through this small garden
in high desert country
where a little water nudges
lantana into prodigious blooms,
yellow, orange, red – and wind
rustles boughs of desert willow
scattering lavender blossoms
into azure skies

I will speak of amazement
as we look beyond stone walls
circling this garden – and gaze
at vast desert expanses
where a jackrabbit races
through an obstacle course
of sage and creosote
while a hawk floats on airy
updrafts, his hungry eyes fixed
on the scene below

Now look with me further
at distant mountains lifting jagged
peaks high above the desert floor –
and I must tell you of the hallelujah
that shakes my soul whenever
I consider the miracle that is us
in a most amazing moment,
here in this stunning cathedral

> God saw everything that he had made,
> and behold, it was very good
> Genesis 1: 31

Psalm 294

My cousin says, "I am certain of two things.
There is a God. I am an agnostic."

"Certain," an unusual term for agnostics,
a crowd that prefers not to come down
on one side or the other of metaphysical
claims.
Perhaps there is a God.
Perhaps not.

Yet my agnostic cousin is certain of God.

He has my full attention.
He is talking about me.
His inner tensions are mine.

I am recalling a line from Tennyson
who reaches toward an equilibrium
"where mind and soul, according well,
may make one music."

My sober head thinks, "Maybe."
Every beat of my heart says, "Yes."

The tightly strung string
of this dialectic sings
one music.

The heart has its reasons
of which reason knows nothing
Blaise Pascal

Psalm 295

I am a watcher of night skies

a wanderer through mysteries of deep space
and ancient texts

a walker of terrestrial trails
where I listen to the silence of flora
the myriad voices of fauna
and songs of the wind

This gives perspective –
vast
long-view, very long
like before history and after,
before our species and after we are gone
or, perhaps, have evolved

Perspective
far different
from the talking heads
who offer up daily headlines and commentary –
short term
sometimes hopeful
often horrifying
always cramped and nearsighted

Yet, perhaps necessary stories
to push us forward
on our circuitous journey
to Teilhard de Chardin's
Omega Point –
or, as prophets have envisioned
for millennia, a new us

> Let justice roll down like waters,
> and righteousness like an everlasting stream
> Amos 5:2

Psalm 296

Three red candles
standing next to each other
in their black cast-iron candelabra

I touch a match to each

One for gratitude
one for mystery
one for love

Gratitude for this crape myrtle
beyond my window, honey bees
probing its pink blossoms –
and yet ten thousand more wonders
in this day inviting hymns of praise

Mystery –
dark matter and dark energy,
95% of the Universe evading our five senses,
yet we are sure it is here – by inference.
God –
unknown to our five senses,
yet inferred by human intuition,
sacred presence of a thousand names

Love –
human capacity to heal our fractured world
if only our politics can be persuaded.
Yet, short of universal blooming,
today a white rose flourishes
in myriad little Edens, pole to pole

Three wicks burning.
One Light
in which to sing
to work
to suffer
to hope
to wait

Sing to the Lord a new song,
God's praise in the assembly of the faithful
Psalm 149: 1

Psalm 297

I number myself
among the fortunate –
the 10% of our world
who have enough

I'm not rich,
as wealth is measured in money,
but I am abundantly blessed
with treasure of family, friends,
education, employment, community,
faith – and enough money

Enough money
is what 90% of my siblings
do not have –
what I would not have
if I had not been born
to the right parents
in the right place
at the right time
with abundant opportunity
and sufficient ambition

I am fortunate, yet distressed
by the haunting eyes of hungry children,
tent cities of refugees, young soldiers
maimed and dead, bombed cities, empty
chairs at the tables of peace and justice

I recall a Sunday evening at church
when my high school quartet sang,
"This world is not my home,
I'm just a passing through"

Fortune has smiled on me.
But I do not feel at home
in this 10% - 90% world

> How shall we sing the Lord's song
> in a foreign land?
> Psalm 137: 4

Psalm 298

Is it possible
I have used up a lifetime
nurturing a friendship
with what is not –

        i.e. God?

Perhaps

Is the oasis in this desert a mirage?
Perhaps
But I drink deeply from its waters

Is the ship on the far horizon a fantasy?
Perhaps
But it carries me to distant ports

Is the city of which I dream a utopian illusion?
Perhaps
But the vision inspires my song

Are the questions that most vex me unanswerable?
Thus far
But they are the most interesting

Is the universal justice that prophets extol beyond our reach?
Yes, for today
But who are we if we do not reach

God has put eternity into our minds,
yet so that we cannot find out what God
has done from the beginning to the end
Ecclesiastes 3: 11

Psalm 299

Sing
people of Earth

Sing lustily

Lift your hearts and voices
into far reaches of our Universe

Let billions upon billions of stars,
and planets with their circling
moons, hear our songs

Boom your music into the fury
of exploding supernova

Fling your harmonies into vast
unknowns beyond farsighted telescopes

Shout triple fortissimo into deep
darkness that surrounds our fragile lights

Chant as though our small species
alone, in all the Universe,
is able to give voice to awe,
terror, amazement and praise

Let your songs, within a nanosecond, fly
Home into the heart of fathomless Mystery

Let our children hear this music
and take their songs beyond ours

> I will sing to God
> who has dealt bountifully with me
> Psalm 13: 6

Psalm 300

Ten thousand psalms chant,
dance and sing within

I have spoken a few
and need not weary you with more

These songs are also in you and you –
singing in us all, as they always have,

beginning with our first parents,
even before they had language

Some translate this music of our depths
into words, harmony and rhythm

These translations are often works
of beauty, but we psalmists know

the lines inscribed on paper barely
hint at what we hear within

Most folks are content – indeed find joy
in mere listening (forget the "mere")

Listening,
prayer's truest form and highest end

With my whole heart I will give you thanks
Psalm 138: 1

INDEX OF REPEATING THEMES

Trust	Question	Quest	Music	Prayer	Celebrate	Universe	Silence
159	151	151	151	154	155	156	154
164	152	152	153	189	157	159	163
168	158	155	157	192	158	167	170
170	159	159	171	193	161	180	171
171	160	160	173	199	162	183	173
172	161	161	182	222	167	190	179
174	168	166	183	224	169	194	181
175	173	170	185	225	172	198	182
179	176	172	188	232	175	200	183
180	177	173	190	239	183	206	191
181	184	177	195	243	188	210	197
182	189	178	196	251	200	210	212
184	192	180	197	253	207	213	225
187	194	182	198	254	220	214	236
201	197	185	203	257	246	217	252
202	205	186	206	258	255	218	253
203	207	195	212	259	260	219	257
210	213	196	215	267	261	222	258
218	216	197	220	271	264	224	272
220	219	205	225	279	265	227	283
221	223	207	236	283	266	228	
223	225	210	239	290	272	229	
227	226	211	240	295	273	230	
231	227	224	244	300	274	237	
232	228	226	247		279	238	
238	231	234	262		296	250	
242	234	235	264		299	262	
244	235	237	282			268	
247	238	240	291			274	
250	241	249	293			295	
251	243	252	294			299	
254	244	267	299				
258	247	269	300				
271	249	271					
272	261	275					
274	262	280					
289	266	286					
290	269	288					
291	274	296					
293	282	298					
294	285						
296	288						
298	289						
	292						

INDEX OF REPEATING THEMES

Lament	Mortality	Wonder	Nature	Home	Jesus	A.M.	P.M.
163	174	153	158	170	166	193	184
165	175	162	175	181	191	195	196
168	194	192	198	190	197	212	199
176	209	204	230	196	226	220	214
178	213	205	231	202	241	246	219
185	229	206	255	203	246	255	
208	230	210	257	221	249	259	
209	231	214	262	236	274	264	
215	245	215	265	249	276	265	
229	256	216	273	253	287	273	
230	268	217	275	255		279	
232	270	219	283	266			
233	275	222	285	297			
239	277	227	293				
248	287	229	295				
254		244					
259		250					
266		255					
278		289					
281		293					
284							
285							
286							
297							

Printed and bound by PG in the USA

USA2018PGIL